THE LIVERPOOL COLLECTION

THE LIVERPOOL COLLECTION

breedon books
PUBLISHING

First published in Great Britain in 2003 by
The Breedon Books Publishing Company Limited
Breedon House, 3 The Parker Centre,
Derby, DE21 4SZ.

ISBN 1 85983 394 2

Printed and bound by Butler & Tanner,
Frome, Somerset, England.

Cover printing by Lawrence-Allen Colour Printers,
Weston-super-Mare, Somerset, England.

Contents

Introduction

IT was in March 1892 that John Houlding, a former lord mayor of Liverpool, was left with a football ground and no team to use it after Everton moved to a new ground at Goodison Park following a dispute with Houlding over the rent at Anfield.

Houlding's solution was simple: he simply founded another club. The FA said that he could not call it 'Everton' because that name belonged to the majority of members who had uprooted to the other side of Stanley Park. Again the answer was simple: he called his new club simply 'Liverpool FC'.

Eventually, Houlding faded from the scene but a prominent local businessman named John McKenna stepped into the void. Initially Liverpool wanted to join the Football League's new Second Division but were rejected. Instead they competed in the Lancashire League and promptly won the championship as well as the Liverpool Cup in their first season. Both trophies were stolen and it cost the new club £130 to replace them.

In 1893 Liverpool were elected to Second Division at the expense of their neighbours, Bootle. In only their second season of existence, they romped to the title, going unbeaten throughout the season, and then – because promotion was not automatic in those days – won a play-off with Newton Heath, later to become Manchester United, to gain entry to the top flight.

In the early years of the 20th century, Liverpool won the League championship twice, played in their first FA Cup Final on the eve of World War One, and then won consecutive League titles again in the early 1920s.

They were the first champions when proper competitive football started up again after World War Two and played in another FA Cup Final in 1950. But that decade was not a happy one for Liverpool FC. Then in December 1959 Bill Shankly took over as manager with the club in the Second Division again.

His appointment heralded an astonishing turnaround. Promotion was followed by three League titlles and a first-ever FA Cup Final success before Shankly retired in 1974. His successor, Bob Paisley, continued to win trophy after trophy, a theme carried on by Joe Fagan and Kenny Dalglish.

By 1992, Liverpool had lifted a record 18 Football League championships, the European Cup four times, the FA Cup five times, and won four consecutive League Cup Finals.

This book covers those first 100 years, looking at the players, the managers and the games. It will both entertain and inform and prove a wonderful souvenir of a great football club.

Early Days

Liverpool, Football League champions, 1900-01. Back row (left to right): Ottey, John Glover, Andy McGuigan, Foster, T.Hunter, John Hunter, 'Rabbi' Howell. Middle row: Soulsby, Charlie Wilson, Sam Raybould, John Robertson, Perkins, Bill Goldie, Maurice Parry. Front row: John Walker, Billy Dunlop, Alex Raisbeck, Jack Cox, Tommy Robertson.

Liverpool, Second Division champions, pictured in 1904-05. Back row (left to right): Maurice Parry, David Murray, Peter Platt, Teddy Doig, Billy Dunlop, Charlie Wilson, C.Evans. Middle row: W.Connell (trainer), George Fleming, James Hughes, John Carlin, Tom Chorlton, Jack Cox, George Lathom, Alex Raisbeck, Tom Watson (secretary). On ground: Arthur Goddard, Robert Robinson, Sam Raybould, Richard Morris, Joe Hewitt, Jack Parkinson, James Garside.

The opening day of the 1905-06 season and Liverpool (white shirts) visit Plumstead to play Woolwich Arsenal. The home side won 3-1 but by the end of the season it was Liverpool who were crowned champions.

Liverpool's playing and training staff pictured in 1905-06, the season the Reds lifted the League championship again. Standing (left to right): W.Connell (trainer), Joe Hewitt, Charlie Wilson, Sam Hardy, Maurice Parry, Teddy Doig, Billy Dunlop, J.Hardy. Seated: Robert Robinson, James Gorman, David Murray, James Hughes, Alex Raisbeck, Jack Cox, George Fleming, Alf West. On ground: Arthur Goddard, George Lathom, John Carlin.

Another Liverpool group from 1905-06 – the title-winning season – this time containing a few more players. Back row (left to right): John Carlin, Alf West, Charlie Wilson, Sam Hardy, Teddy Doig, Billy Dunlop, David Murray, Joe Hewitt. Middle row: W.Connell (trainer), James Hughes, George Lathom, John Hughes, Maurice Parry, Alex Raisbeck, George Fleming, Tom Chorlton, Tom Watson (secretary). Front row: G. Robinson, James Gorman, Arthur Goddard, Robert Robinson, Jack Parkinson, Sam, Raybould, Jack Cox, James Garside.

Liverpool's playing and training staff pictured in 1908-09. Back row (left to right): Arthur Goddard, Grantham, James Bradley, Joe Hewitt, E.Hughes, George Lathom, Jimmy Harrop. Middle row: W.Connell (trainer), Sam Hardy, Robert Robinson, Percy Saul, Maurice Parry, Donald Sloan, Jack Parkinson, Tom Rogers, George Fleming (trainer). Seated: Dick Allman, F.Smith, Michael Griffen, Billy Dunlop, Alex Raisbeck, Bert Goode, James Hughes, Ronald Orr, Alf West. On ground: Tom Chorlton, Ernest Peake, Sam Bowyer. The Reds finished 16th in Division One.

Liverpool's playing and training staff pictured in 1909-10, the season they finished League championship runners-up. Back row (left to right): Sam Bowyer, John McDonald, Harold Uren, Robert Robinson, John McCornell, William McPherson. Middle row: Augustus Beeby, Jack Parkinson, Dillon, Tom Chorlton, Jimmy Harrop, J.Dunlop. Seated: George Fleming (trainer), Tom Rogers, Robert Crawford, Arthur Goddard, Billy Dunlop, James Bradley, Joe Hewitt, Alan Hignett, W.Connell (trainer). On ground ground: Ernest Peake, Ronald Orr, Lawson, Bert Goode, Richard Morris, Stuart.

A scramble for the ball at Stamford Bridge in October 1913 when Liverpool went down 3-0 to Chelsea in a First Division match. At the end of the season Liverpool finished 16th, but reached the FA Cup Final for the first time.

Sam Hardy made 239 League and FA Cup appearances for Liverpool after joining the Reds from Chesterfield in 1905. One of the outstanding goalkeepers of the 1900s, he won 21 England caps and altogether made 552 League appearances in a career which also took in Aston Villa and Nottingham Forest.

Full-back Eph Longworth was the first Liverpool player to skipper England. The Reds signed him from Bolton Wanderers in 1910 and by the time he retired in 1928 he had made 370 League and FA Cup appearances for Liverpool, played in the 1914 Cup Final, won two championship medals and five England caps.

Ten of the Liverpool team which appeared in the 1914 FA Cup Final, when they lost 1-0 to Burnley at the Crystal Palace. Back row (left to right): Thomas Fairfoul, Harry Lowe, Eph Longworth, Kenneth Campbell, Bob Pursell, Robert Ferguson. Front row: Donald McKinlay, Arthur Metcalfe, Tom Miller, Billy Lacey, Jackie Sheldon.

Goalkeeper Kenneth Campbell joined Liverpool from Cambuslang in 1911 and won his chance when Sam Hardy moved to Aston Villa. Campbell made 142 League and FA Cup appearances for Liverpool before being transferred to Partick Thistle in 1920 after losing his place to Elisha Scott. He won eight Scottish caps and played in the 1914 FA Cup Final.

Billy Lacey joined from Everton in February 1912. An Irish international – he won 23 caps – he played in the 1914 FA Cup Final and in both title-winning seasons after World War One. He moved to New Brighton in 1924, after 257 League and FA Cup appearances for Liverpool, and 29 goals.

Liverpool, 1914-15, the last season before the Football League was suspended because of World War One. Back row (left to right): Thomas Fairfoul, Harry Lowe, John Speakman, Kenneth Campbell, Bob Pursell, Donald McKinlay, Robert Ferguson. Front row: Jackie Sheldon, Arthur Metcalfe, Robert McDougall, Billy Lacey, Jimmy Nicholl.

Fred Pagnam made only 39 senior appearances for Liverpool but he scored 30 goals in that time. Joining the Reds from Blackpool in October 1914, he scored on his debut and then hit four in his next game. In his first season he top-scored with 24 in 29 League games. Just how many her would have scored had war not intervened is open to debate but in 1919-20 he netted four times in eight games before being transferred to Cardiff City. In 1922-23, when he was with Watford, he was the leading scorer in the Third Division South with 30 goals.

Outside-right Jackie Sheldon joined Liverpool from Manchester United in 1913, played in the 1914 FA Cup Final and was then suspended after contriving the result of a match against his former club on Good Friday 1915, by missing a penalty. The suspension was subsequently lifted and Sheldon was a regular in the first seasons after World War One.

Between Two Wars

Liverpool's 1921-22 League championship-winning team. Back row (left to right): W Connell (trainer), Harry Chambers, Jock McNab, Elisha Scott, Walter Wadsworth, Tommy Bromilow, Dick Forshaw. Middle row: Dave Ashworth (manager), Billy Lacey, Eph Longworth, Donald McKinlay, Tommy Lucas, Fred Hopkin, George Patterson (secretary). Front row: Danny Shone, Harry Lewis.

Wing-half Tommy Bromilow won five England caps and made 374 League and FA Cup appearances for Liverpool between 1919-20 and 1929-30. He missed only three games in the two title-winning seasons of 1921-2-3.

Harry Chambers scored 41 goals for Liverpool in the two title-winning seasons of the early 1920s. Altogether he made 338 League and FA Cup appearances for the Reds, scoring 151 goals, before moving to West Brom in 1928.

Winger Fred Hopkin joined Liverpool from Manchester United in 1921 and scored only 11 goals in 359 League and FA Cup appearances for Liverpool. But his first-ever goal for the club – against Bolton in March 1923 – was special: a fire immediately broke out in the main stand at Anfield! He missed only two games in the championship-winning seasons of 1921-2-3.

Dick Johnson scored 30 goals in 83 League and FA Cup appearances for Liverpool in the seasons immediately after World War One. Injury meant that he missed the first championship-winning season of 1921-22, but he netted 14 times in 37 games in the second. Eventually injury forced his retirement.

Full-back Tommy Lucas signed from Manchester United in 1919 and made 366 League and FA Cup appearances for Liverpool before retiring in 1933. He was capped three times for England and played in the first championship-winning season but made only one appearance in the second.

Donald McKinlay was a utility player who spent 19 years with Liverpool, making 433 League and FA Cup appearances for the Reds. He joined them from Scottish junior football in 1909 and stayed until 1929 when his first-class career was over because on an injury and he signed for Prescot Cables. McKinlay played in the 1914 Cup Final, skippered the Reds in their two title-winning seasons of the 1920s and won two Scotland caps.

Jock McNab, a wing-half, won his first-team place at Liverpool for the title-winning season of 1921-22 and missed only three games when the championship was retained the following season. He made 221 first-team appearances for the Reds and was capped for Scotland against Wales in 1923. He left for QPR in the close season of 1928.

Elisha Scott kept goal for Liverpool on no less then 467 occasions between 1913 and 1934. He won championship medals in 1921-22 and 1922-23 and was capped 31 times for Ireland, his last international appearance coming when he was 42. One reporter wrote: "He has the eye of an eagle, the movement of a panther, the clutch of a vice."

Harry Wadsworth was a winger who made 54 League appearances for Liverpool in the seasons after World War One. He was the brother of Walter Wadsworth, who made 240 senior appearances for Liverpool before and after the war. The pair played together in the championship-winning seasons of 1921-2-3.

Liverpool parade the League championship trophy in 1922. Charlie Wilson (holding the trophy) and Andy McGuigan (seated) both appeared in the 1900-01 championship-winning team.

Liverpool's players and staff pictured with the Football League championship trophy which the club won for the fourth time – and the second time in succession – in 1922-23.

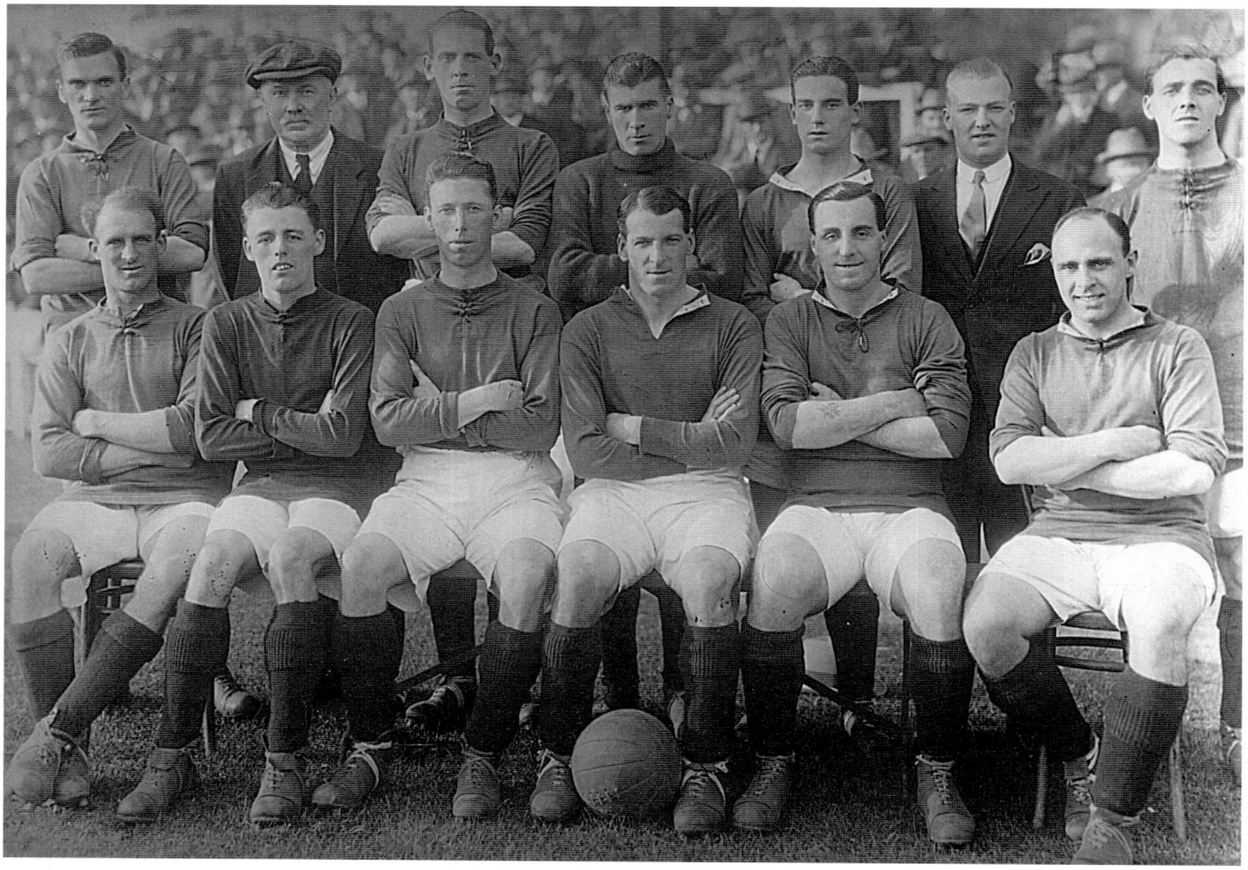

Liverpool pictured early in the 1923-24 season. Back row (left to right): Walter Wadsworth, W.Connell (trainer), Jock McNab, Elisha Scott, Jimmy Walsh, unknown, Tom Bromilow. Front row: Eph Longworth, Cyril Gilhespy, Dick Forshaw, Donald McKinlay, Harry Chambers, Fred Hopkin.

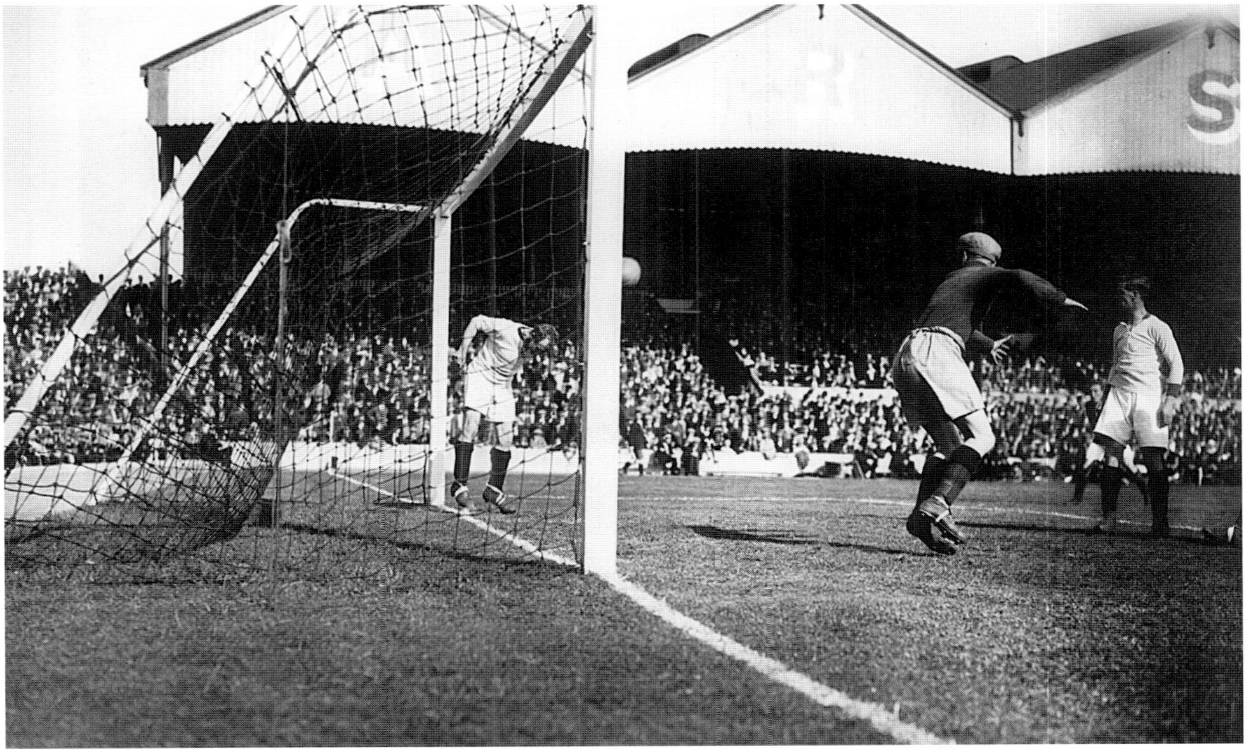

With Liverpool goalkeeper Arthur Riley beaten, Eph Longworth heads a shot from Arsena 's Jimmy Brain off the goa -l ne at Highbury in September 1926. Liverpool, though, lost 2-0.

Arsenal's Charlie Buchan is beaten to the ball by Liverpool's Albert Shears.

West Ham goalkeeper David Baillie attempts to block a shot from Liverpool's Jimmy McDougall at Upton Park in October 1928 but the ball found its way into the net for the only goal of the game.

Gordon Hodgson arrived in England with a South African touring party and stayed behind to sign for Liverpool in 1925. He quickly made the transition and when he moved to Leeds United ten years later had scored 240 goals in 378 League and FA Cup matches for the Reds.

Jimmy McDougall signed for Liverpool from Partick Thistle in the summer of 1928 and went on to make 357 senior appearances for the Reds. Originally an inside-forward, McDougall was moved to left-half and that was his position for the next ten seasons. He was capped twice for Scotland and left Anfield for South Liverpool in 1938.

Liverpool skipper Jimmy Jackson (right) meets his Everton counterpart Hunter Hart before a Merseyside derby at Anfield in February 1929.

Action from a pre-season public practice match at Anfield in August 1929. The goalkeeper is the South African-born Arthur Riley, who was the regular first-team choice that season.

Liverpool, 1932-33. Back row (left to right): Mr Asbury (director), Norman James, Jimmy McDougall, Gordon Hodgson, Elisha Scott, Tom Morrison, Mr Williams, trainer, Mr W.H. Cartwright (chairman). Front row: Robert Done, Willie Steele, Harold Barton, Tom Bradshaw, Vic Wright, Gordon Gunson, Syd Roberts.

Liverpool, 1935-36. Back row (left to right): Jim Harley, Ben Dabbs, Arthur Riley, Bob Savage, Jimmy McDougall. Front row: James Collins, Jack Balmer, Tom Bradshaw, Fred Howe, Ted Hartill, Vic Wright.

Liverpool Reserves, 1935-36. Back row (left to right): Fred Rogers, Norman Low, Ben Dabbs, Mr Williams (director), Stan Kane, Felton, John Browning, Eph Longworth (trainer). Front row: Guy, Neale, Jack Balmer, Tom Bush, Bob Glassey, Alf Hanson.

Liverpool, 1936-37. Back row (left to right): Mr W.H. Cartwright (director), Berry Nieuwerhuys, Ben Dabbs, Mr G. Richards (director), Alf Hobson, Matt Busby, Fred Rogers, Mr W.J. Harrop (chairman). Front row: Tom Bush, Harry Eastham, Tommy Cooper, Jack Balmer, Alf Hanson.

Alf Hobson, the Liverpool goalkeeper, hugs the ball on the goal-line as Stan Prior, the Charlton forward, stands over him. The Liverpool defenders are Tom Bradshaw (right) and Tommy Cooper. The sides drew 1-1 at the Valley in September 1936.

Whoops! Liverpool goalkeeper Arthur Riley fumbles a shot from Alf Kirchen and Arsenal score the winning goal in the League match at Highbury in March 1937. The crowd was just over 16,000.

Liverpool, 1937-38. Back row (left to right): John Browning, Tom Bush, Matt Busby, Arthur Riley, Phil Taylor, Jim Harley, Ben Dabbs. Front row: Berry Nieuwenhuys, John Shafto, Tommy Cooper, Willie Fagan, Fred Rogers, Alf Hanson.

Liverpool, 1938-39, the last full season before League football was suspended because of World War Two. Back row (left to right): Tom Bush, Matt Busby, Phil Taylor, Arthur Riley, Charlie Wilson (trainer), Fred Rogers, Jim Harley, G.H.Richards (director). Front row: Berry Nieuwenhuys, Jack Balmer, Tommy Cooper, Mr W.J. Harrop (chairman), Jimmy McInnes, Willie Fagan, Harman Van Den Berg.

Roaring Forties

Liverpool, 1946-47, first League champions of the post-war era. Back row (left to right): Tom Bush, Phil Taylor, Jim Harley, Cyril Sidlow, Ray Lambert, Bob Paisley, A.Shelley (trainer). Front row: William Watkinson, Willie Fagan, Albert Stubbins, Stan Polk, Billy Liddell, Laurie Hughes

Liverpool, 1949-50. Back row (left to right): George Kay (manager), Phil Taylor, Ray Lambert, Cyril Sidlow, Bob Paisley, Eddie Spicer, A.Shelley (trainer). Front row: Jimmy Payne, Kevin Baron, Cyril Done, Willie Fagan, Billy Liddell, Laurie Hughes.

Bob Paisley, followed by Laurie Hughes. Paisley signed for Liverpool before World War two but had to wait until 1946 for his League debut. He made 278 senior appearances at wing-half before retiring in 1954. Paisley joined the Reds' backroom staff and eventually replaced Bill Shankly after his shock resignation in 1974. Paisley proved an even more successful manager than his predecessor, leading the Reds to an unprecedented array of domestic and European honours.

Arsenal defender Laurie Scott is left floundering by Liverpool's Scottish international winger Billy Liddell. Nearly 56,000 saw this First Division match at Highbury in September 1949, which the Merseysiders won 2-1.

Laurie Scott (2) looks behind him as Liverpool's Willie Fagan gets in a spectacular flying header. Joe Mercer is behind Fagan.

In 1950, there was an all-Merseyside FA Cup semi-final staged at Maine Road, when Liverpool won 2-0. This picture shows Liverpool's second goal scored by Billy Liddell (not in picture). The hapless Everton defenders are goalkeeper George Burnett, left-back Jack Hedley and inside-right Eddie Wainwright (8).

Liverpool goalkeeper Cyril Sidlow and his defenders are in a terrible tangle during the 1950 FA Cup Final against Arsenal.

Leslie Compton hammers the ball away from Liverpool's Albert Stubbins. Arsenal's Wally Barnes and Joe Mercer are in the background.

Peter Goring is just beaten to the ball by Sidlow.

Swindin, Barnes and company watch as Stubbins fails to connect with the ball.

The Wolves defence foils Jimmy Payne at Anfield in December 1950. Len Gibbons is the defender fending off Payne as goalkeeper Dennis Parsons collects the ball. Wolves won 4-1.

Arsenal's Leslie Compton and Liverpool's Albert Stubbins in action at Highbury in April 1951. Liverpool won 2-1 before a 42,000 crowd.

Liverpool's Albert Stubbins slides in but Chelsea goalkeeper Bill Robertson appears to have got the ball away at Stamford Bridge in August 1951. Liverpool won 3-1.

Arsenal centre-forward Cliff Holton runs in as Liverpool goalkeeper Charlie Ashcroft gathers the ball safely at Highbury in September 1951. The sides drew 0-0 in front of a 50,000 crowd.

Derby goalkeeper Ray Middleton punches clear from Billy Liddell at Anfield in September 1951. The Reds won 2-0 in front of 40,259 spectators.

Billy Liddell was the greatest name in Liverpool's immediate post-war story. He signed for the Reds before the war, in which he served as an RAF navigator, and made his first-team debut when peace was restored in 1945. Liddell played in 537 senior games and scored 229 goals. He was capped 28 times for Scotland and played for the Great Britain against the Rest of the World twice. After his retirement in 1961 he became bursar at Liverpool University and a JP.

Jimmy Payne's shot spills out of Chelsea goalkeeper Bill Robertson's hands at Anfield in December 1951. The sides drew 1-1 before 26,459 spectators.

This time it is the turn of Portsmouth goalkeeper Ernie Butler to get in the way of a Jimmy Payne shot. Nearly 50,000 fans saw this 1-1 draw at Anfield in September 1952.

Fifties Doldrums

Liverpool, 1953-54, the season they were relegated after finishing bottom of Division One. Back row (left to right): Phil Taylor (manager), Ray Lambert, Laurie Hughes, Russell Crossley, A.Shelley (trainer), Eddie Spicer, Billy Liddell, Jimmy Payne. Front row: Roy Saunders, Brian Jackson, Bill Jones, Louis Bimpson, Alan A'Court, Joe Maloney.

Louis Bimpson scores his and Liverpool's third goal against Burnley at Anfield in September 1953. Bimpson added another and the Reds won 4-0 in front of 36,643 spectators.

Louis Bimpson scored 40 goals in 100 League and FA Cup games for Liverpool after joining the club from Burscough and making his debut in March 1953. He was joint top scorer in 1953-54, when he scored all four goals against Burnley. Bimpson left Anfield for Blackburn Rovers in 1959.

Spurs goalkeeper Ted Ditchburn and right-back Alf Ramsay hold up Alan A'Court and Eric Anderson at Anfield in January 1954. The game ended 2-2; the attendance was 43,592.

Alan A'Court made his mark at Anfield as a speedy winger. Singed from Prescot Cables, he made his debut in 1953 and by the time he left for Tranmere in 1964 had made 382 senior appearances and scored 63 goals for the Reds. He won five England caps.

On the opening day of the 1955-56 season, Liverpool won 3-1 at Nottingham Forest in the Second Division. Here Reds' goalkeeper Doug Rudham punches clear from Forest's Peter Higham. A crowd of 21,389 was at the City Ground.

Liverpool-born Ronnie Moran joined his local club as a 17-year-old full-back in 1952 and made his League debut in November that year. Despite injury problems in his career, he had played in 379 first-team games and scored 16 goals before retiring in 1965 to join the backroom staff at Anfield. In 1992 he took over as temporary manager when Graeme Souness underwent major heart surgery.

Ronnie Moran heads clear against Plymouth Argyle at Anfield in October 1955. Liverpool won 4-1. A crowd of 34,397 was present.

Alan A'Court scores one of his two goals against Plymouth. At the end of the 1955-56 season, Plymouth were relegated to the Third Division South.

On 7 January 1956, Liverpool beat Accrington Stanley 2-0 in the third round of the FA Cup in front of 48,385 fans. Here, Dave Underwood, the Liverpool goalkeeper, is under pressure from the Third Division North side.

Alan Arnell scores Liverpool's second goal, from Alan A'Court's pass, against Leicester City at Anfield in January 1956. Nearly 40,000 saw the Reds win 3-1.

Ronnie Moran heads the ball for a corner before Stoke's Neville Coleman can get to it at the Victoria Ground in January 1957. Goalkeeper Tommy Younger looks on anxiously. The Potters won 1-0.

Goalkeeper Tommy Younger joined Liverpool from Hibernian in 1956, for £9,000. He made 127 League and FA Cup appearances before becoming player-manager of Falkirk in 1959. He was capped 24 times for Scotland, 16 of them whilst with Liverpool.

In January 1957 Liverpool were on the wrong end of an FA Cup shock when Third Division South club Southend United beat them 2-1 at Roots Hall in the third round. The Reds eventually gained their revenge the following year, beating Southend 3-2 after a third-round replay. Here the Reds defence are helpless as Southend score their winner in the first tie.

Liverpool's Tony Rowley scored twice in the 2-1 win against Port Vale at Vale Park in March 1957 but on this occasion Vale goalkeeper Ray King just got to the ball before Rowley.

Tony Rowley was on target again the following week, when Liverpool beat Rotherham United 4-1 at Anfield. Here Rowley clatters into the Rotherham goalkeeper, Roy Ironside.

In November 1958, Liverpool lost 3-2 at Derby after goalkeeper Tommy Younger hurt his back while trying to clear from the Rams forward George Darwin in the incident pictured here.

Younger is helped from the Baseball Ground pitch. Amazingly, fans have got on to the pitch and the optimistic youngster on the left of the picture appears hopeful of an autograph. Younger returned to play at centre-forward.

Liverpool, 1957-58. Back row (left to right): John Molyneux, Johnny Wheeler, Tommy Younger, Laurie Hughes, Ronnie Moran, Don Campbell. Front row: Brian Jackson, Tony Rowley, Billy Liddell, John Evans, Alan A'Court.

A seven-goal thriller against Leyton Orient at Anfield in November 1959, with the Reds just edging both points. Here Liverpool goalkeeper Bert Slater grabs the ball as the Os' centre-forward Tom Johnston (9) get in a challenge.

Shankly Revival

The legendary Bill Shankly points the way. After a distinguished playing career with Preston North End – when he won five Scotland caps – Shankly managed Carlisle, Grimsby, Workington and Huddersfield before taking over at Anfield in December 1959. Seldom, if ever, can the arrival of a manager have changed so completely the fortunes of a football club. He took them from the Second Division to League championships, FA Cup and UEFA Cup triumphs and set in motion the most glorious era in the Reds' history.

Billy Liddell (out of picture) scores his last goal for Liverpool, against Stoke City at Anfield in March 1960. The Reds won 5-1.

Roger Hunt watches his effort hit the back of the Middlesbrough net at Ayresome Park in January 1960. Liverpool fought back to draw 3-3. Hunt had scored on his League debut for Liverpool, after signing in 1959 after National Service in the Army. He holds several club records including most League goals in a season (41 in 1961-62) and most League goals overall (245). Hunt was capped 34 times for England, including the 1966 World Cup Final, and scored 18 goals for his country. He moved to Bolton Wanderers in 1969.

Dave Hickson goes near with a header against Derby at Anfield in October 1960. A crowd of 24,659 saw Liverpool win 1-0.

Ronnie Moran (with Jimmy Melia on his left and Alan A'Court to his right) acknowledges the Anfield crowd after the Reds beat Southampton 2-0 at Anfield in April 1962, to ensure promotion back to the top flight.

Liverpool goalkeeper Jim Furnell is beaten by a header from Manchester City's Neil Young at Maine Road in August 1962. The game ended 2-2.

This time Peter Dobing beats Furnell with a low shot. Ron Yeats and Gerry Byrne are also left stranded.

Bolton's Eddie Hopkinson grabs the ball from Roger Hunt at Anfield in October 1962. Hunt scored the only goal of the game.

West Ham's Martin Peters gets the ball away from Roger Hunt as the Hammers' goalkeeper Jim Standen rushes out at Anfield in September 1963. Hunt scored in the game but the Hammers won 2-1.

Ron Yeats made 451 appearances (only one of them as a substitute) at the heart of Liverpool's defence from 1961-62 to 1970-71. He was signed from Dundee United, for £30,000 in July 1961, and helped the Reds to an immediate promotion to the top flight. He played twice for Scotland and left Anfield in 1971 to become player-manager of Tranmere Rovers.

Ian St John and Derby's Phil Waller both jump for the ball at Anfield during the FA Cup third-round tie in January 1964. The Reds won 5-0, a victory enjoyed by the overwhelming majority of a 46,460 crowd.

Alf Arrowsmith's shot is smothered by Manchester United goalkeeper Harry Gregg at Anfield in April 1964. Arrowsmith scored twice in Liverpool's 3-0 win.

When Ian St John signed for Liverpool from Motherwell in 1961, he was the Reds' record signing. St John scored 118 goals in 424 first-team games for Liverpool, and altogether won 21 caps for Scotland. In 1971 he went to play in South Africa, later returning to manage Motherwell and Portsmouth and then forging a new career in television.

Ian St John and Manchester United's Harry Gregg are grounded as United's Bill Foulkes races in. Peter Thompson of Liverpool is on the right of the picture.

Geoff Strong cost Liverpool £40,000 when Bill Shankly signed him from Arsenal in 1964. In his first season his only FA Cup appearance came in the Final. After 198 first-team games and 32 goals, Strong moved to Coventry City in 1970.

Peter Thompson scored 54 goals in 412 games on Liverpool's left wing. He joined the Reds from Preston for £35,000 in 1963. Ten years later he moved to Bolton Wanderers. Thompson was capped 16 times for England.

Bobby Graham scored a hat-trick on his League debut for Liverpool, against Aston Villa in September 1964. Motherwell-born, he joined Liverpool as an apprentice in 1961 and went on to make 131 senior appearances, scoring 42 goals, before moving to Coventry in 1972.

Villa's Charlie Aitken could not prevent Roger Hunt's header from finding the back of the net at Anfield in September 1964, but the Liverpool man's effort was ruled offside. Liverpool, though, won the game 5-1 with Tony Hateley getting Villa's consolation.

Ian St John leaps to head Liverpool's final goal in their 4-2 win over Sheffield Wednesday at Anfield in January 1965.

Liverpool pictured before the 1965 FA Cup Final. Back row (left to right): Gordon Milne, Gerry Byrne, Tommy Lawrence, Ron Yeats, Chris Lawler, Willie Stevenson. Front row: Ian Callaghan, Roger Hunt, Ian St John, Tommy Smith, Peter Thompson.

Ian Callaghan made a staggering 848 senior appearances for Liverpool between his debut in 1959-60 and his last season for the Reds in 1977-78, after which he signed for John Toshack's Swansea City. He was capped four times for England, in 1966 and 1977.

Tommy Lawrence signed professional forms for Liverpool in 1957 but had to wait until 1962-63 for his League debut. Thereafter he was an automatic choice until Ray Clemence took over in 1970. He won three Scotland caps and after 387 senior appearances for the Reds he moved to Tranmere Rovers in 1971.

Willie Stevenson was bought from Glasgow Rangers, where he was in the reserves, for £7,000 in 1962. A creative midfielder, Stevenson made 238 senior appearances and scored 17 goals before being transferred to Stoke City at the end of 1967.

Ian St John (extreme left) has just scored Liverpool's third goal against Inter Milan in the 1965 European Cup semi-final first leg at Anfield. Liverpool won 3-1 but lost the tie 4-3 on aggregate after being soundly beaten in Italy.

Tommy Smith was born a few hundred yards from Anfield and joined the groundstaff in 1960. He signed professional forms on his 17th birthday and went on to make 633 first-team appearances as the team's midfield 'iron man', scoring 48 goals. Capped once by England, Smith moved to Swansea City in 1978.

Liverpool-born Gerry Byrne had the misfortune to put through his own goal on his debut in 1957 but went on to make 330 senior appearances as one of the finest full-backs ever to play for Liverpool. He won promotion with the club in 1961-62, played in two championship-winning teams and was a hero of the 1965 FA Cup Final when he laid on a goal for Roger Hunt despite having broken his collar-bone in the opening minutes. He was capped twice for England.

Gordon Milne heads Liverpool's third goal in their 4-1 win over Blackpool at Anfield in February 1966. Tony Waiters is the Seasiders' goalkeeper.

Roger Hunt and Ian St John pictured at Craven Cottage in February 1966 – don't be misled by the Bolton Wanderers flag; in those days Fulham flew flags for all First Division clubs. The Cottagers won 2-0.

Gordon Milne swings on the netting in jubilation after Roger Hunt's 69th-minute winner against Chelsea at Anfield in April 1966. In front of a crowd of 53,754, the Reds won 2-1 to clinch the League championship. It was a remarkable feat. Using only 14 players all season, they went to the top of the table before Christmas, lost only two of their last 19 games and enjoyed their best defensive record since 1922-23, when they also won the title.

Chris Lawler scored 61 goals for Liverpool, a remarkable figure for a full-back. He signed for the club as a junior in 1961 and made 546 senior appearances, winning four England caps, before joining Portsmouth, where Ian St John was manager, in 1975.

Liverpool are in disarray as Celtic's Bobby Lennox (extreme left of the picture) celebrates his goal at Parkhead in the first leg of the 1966 European Cup-winners' Cup semi-final. But Liverpool won the second leg at Anfield 2-0, to go through 2-1 on aggregate. In the Final they lost 2-1 after extra-time to Borussia Dortmund at Hampden Park.

Liverpool in August 1966, about to defend their League championship title. Back row (left to right): Gordon Milne, Gerry Byrne, Tommy Lawrence, Ron Yeats, Chris Lawler, Willie Stevenson. Front row: Ian Callaghan, Roger Hunt, Ian St John, Tommy Smith, Peter Thompson.

Ian St John's shot is blocked by Aston Villa goalkeeper Colin Withers at Anfield in February 1967. Gordon Milne scored the only goal of the game.

Roger Hunt tries a brave header as Tottenham's Pat Jennings tries to lash the ball clear with his boot at Anfield in May 1967, Dave Mackay and Ian St John are close to the action. The game ended goalless.

Roger Hunt heads home against Leicester at Anfield in October 1967 but his effort is disallowed for offside. It was a costly decision as the Reds went on to lose 2-1.

Ron Yeats and Wolves' John Farrington in action at Anfield in November 1967. The Reds won 2-1.

The two Tommies – Smith and Lawrence – both look fed up and no wonder. Howard Kendall, not in the picture), has just scored against the Reds at Goodison in February 1968. It was the only goal of the game.

Peter Thompson rushes in as Leeds United goalkeeper David Harvey collects the ball at Anfield in May 1968. Roger Hunt and Billy Bremner look on. Liverpool won 2-1.

Tony Hateley, who scored a hat-trick that afternoon, heads goalwards against Nottingham Forest at Anfield in May 1968. Forest goalkeeper Mike Harby and Henry Newton guard the goal-line. Liverpool won 6-1.

Liverpool, 1968-69. Back row (left to right): Geoff Strong, Ray Clemence, Tommy Lawrence, Gerry Byrne. Middle row: Bobby Graham, Tony Hateley, Peter Wall, Ian Ross, Alf Arrowsmith, Peter Thompson. Front row: Ian Callaghan, Emlyn Hughes, Roger Hunt, Ron Yeats, Ian St John, Tommy Smith, Chris Lawler.

Ray Clemence made 656 first-team appearances in Liverpool's goal between 1968-69 and 1980-81, when he movec to Spurs for £300,000. Bill Shankly signed Clemence from Scunthorpe United and was understudy to Tommy Lawrence for two seasons. He played in the Reds' first three European Cup Finals and altogether was capped 61 times for England.

Emlyn Hughes made 657 senior appearances for Liverpool, scoring 48 goals. He joined the Reds from Blackpool in 1967, for £65,000, and went on to win 62 England caps. Hughes joined Wolves in 1979. An adaptable player, he was one of the key figures in Liverpool's success in the 1970s.

Arsenal's David Jenkins and Liverpool's Chris Lawler both seem to have missed the ball at Highbury in August 1968. The sides drew 1-1. At the end of the season Liverpool were second, Arsenal fourth.

Ian Callaghan beats Sunderland goalkeeper Jim Montgomery for the Reds' third goal at Anfield in August 1968. Tony Hateley added another and Liverpool won 4-1.

Chris Lawler climbs high to challenge Chelsea's Peter Bonetti at Anfield in November 1968. The Reds won 2-1.

Alun Evans is beaten in the air by Tottenham's Alan Mullery at Anfield in December 1968. An Emlyn Hughes goal settled the issue, 1-0 in Liverpool's favour. Roger Hunt, Phil Beal and Mike England look on.

In April 1969 Liverpool met Leeds United at Anfield in a vital League game. Both sides were vying for the championship but a goalless draw virtually settled the issue in Leeds' favour and they went on to win the title six points ahead of Liverpool. Here, Eddie Gray braces himself as Tommy Smith moves in.

Geoff Strong slides in but Jack Charlton gets his cross over.

Ron Yeats (5) leaps into the arms of goalscorer Geoff Strong after Strong's 60th-minute goal against Chelsea at Anfield in August 1969. Bobby Graham rushes up to join in the celebrations. The Londoners were hammered 4-1.

Tommy Lawrence is not going to save this diving header from Derby's Kevin Hector at the Baseball Ground in November 1969. Nearly 41,000 saw Derby win 4-0.

Ray Clemence saves from the feet of Joe Royle in the November 1970 Merseyside derby game at Anfield, which Liverpool won 3-2.

Alun Evans challenges Bayern Munich goalkeeper Sepp Maier during the Fairs Cup fourth-round first-leg tie at Anfield in March 1971. Liverpool won 3-0 on the night and 4-1 on aggregate but lost to Leeds United in the semi-final.

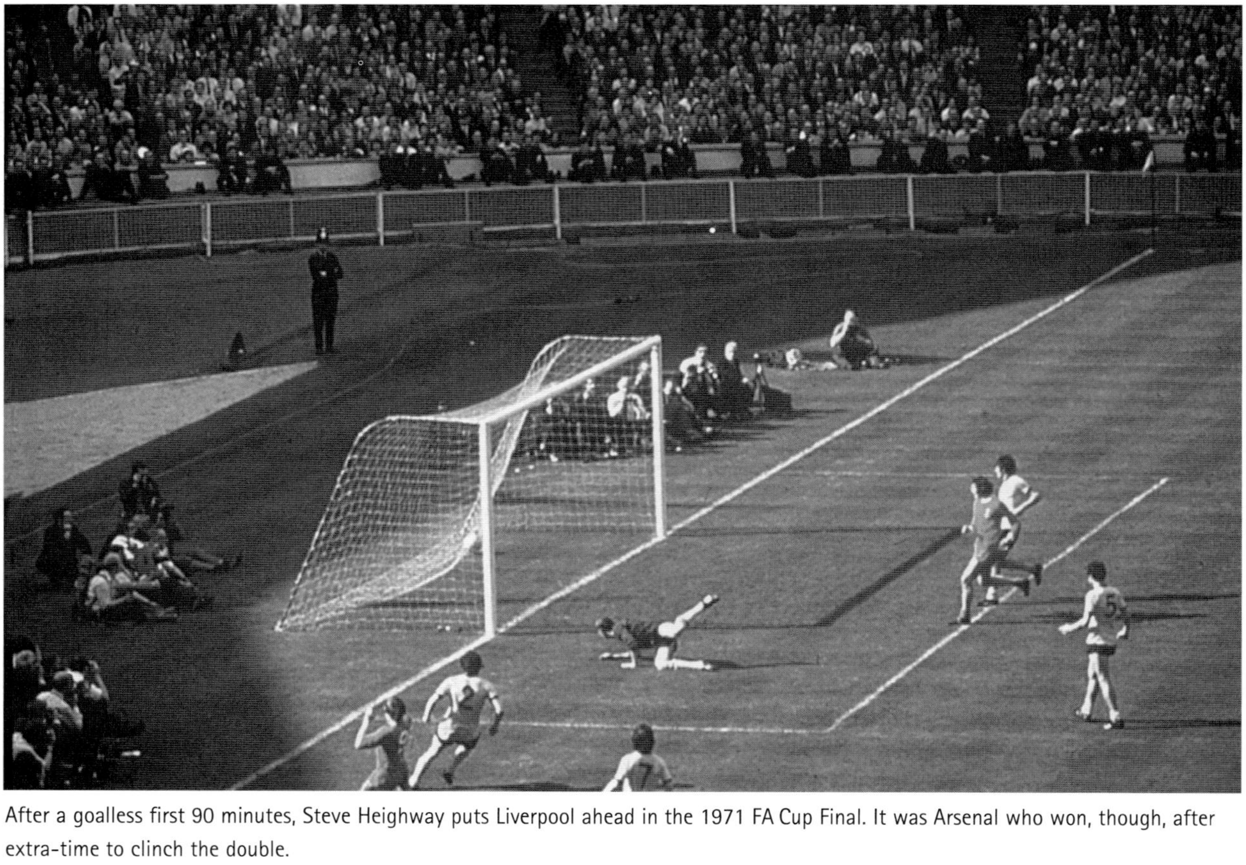

After a goalless first 90 minutes, Steve Heighway puts Liverpool ahead in the 1971 FA Cup Final. It was Arsenal who won, though, after extra-time to clinch the double.

Steve Heighway made his League debut for Liverpool in 1970-71 and went on to play in 467 senior games, scoring 76 goals, before going to play in the United States. Born in Dublin, although his father was English and he lived in England from the age of ten, Heighway opted to play for the Republic, for whom he was capped 34 times, the last cap coming after he had signed for Minnesota Kicks.

Kevin Keegan scored exactly 100 goals in 321 first-team appearances for Liverpool, who he joined from Fourth Division Scunthorpe United for £35,000 in 1971. He won 63 full caps for England and skippered his country. Keegan left Anfield for SV Hamburg in 1977. He returned to play for Southampton and Newcastle and eventually went into management, not least as boss of the England team.

Kevin Keegan has just scored Liverpool's second goal against Leicester City at Anfield in August 1971. John Toshack bends over the goalscorer whilst Peter Shilton can only wonder who to blame. Liverpool won 3-2 and it was Toshack who hit their third.

Welsh international John Toshack scored 95 goals in 245 senior games for Liverpool after joining the Reds from Cardiff City, for £110,000 in 1970. He struck up a great understanding with Kevin Keegan in the Reds' attack in the 1970s. Toshack left Anfield in 1978 to become Swansea City's player-manager. He signed a few of his former Liverpool colleagues and guided the Swans from the old Fourth Division to the First. Toshack later worked successfully as a manager in Spanish football.

Kevin Keegan watches his diving header beat Coventry goalkeeper Bill Glazier to open the scoring at Anfield in April 1972. Liverpool went on to win 3-1.

Ipswich Town goalkeeper David Best clears from John Toshack and Steve Heighway at Anfield in April 1972. Toshack scored both goals in Liverpool's 2-0 win.

Standing 6ft 2in, Larry Lloyd won most of the aerial battles he was involved in. Bill Shankly signed him from Bristol Rovers in 1969, for £60,000 and he made 217 senior appearances before being transferred to Coventry in 1974. Lloyd, who won four England caps, later won further European club honours under Brian Clough at Forest.

On a balmy May evening in 1972, Liverpool arrived at the Baseball Ground with an excellent chance of taking the League championship. A goal from Derby's John McGovern, however, won the game for the Rams who were crowned champions the following week when both Liverpool and Leeds fell at the final hurdle. Here, Ray Clemence looks back to see McGovern's shot on its way into the net.

The race is on between Arsenal's colourful winger Peter Marinello and Liverpool's Steve Heighway at Highbury in September 1972. Over 47,000 saw a goalless draw. At the end of the season Liverpool were champions, Arsenal runners-up three points behind.

Chris Lawler hooks the ball goalwards as the AEK Athens 'keeper dives to block it. Liverpool won this 1971-72 UEFA Cup second-round tie 6-1 on aggregate and went on to lift the trophy by beating Borussia Moenchengladbach 3-2 on aggregate the following May.

Tommy Smith missed this penalty against Newcastle United at Anfield in November 1972 but the Reds still went on to win 3-2.

Onward with Paisley

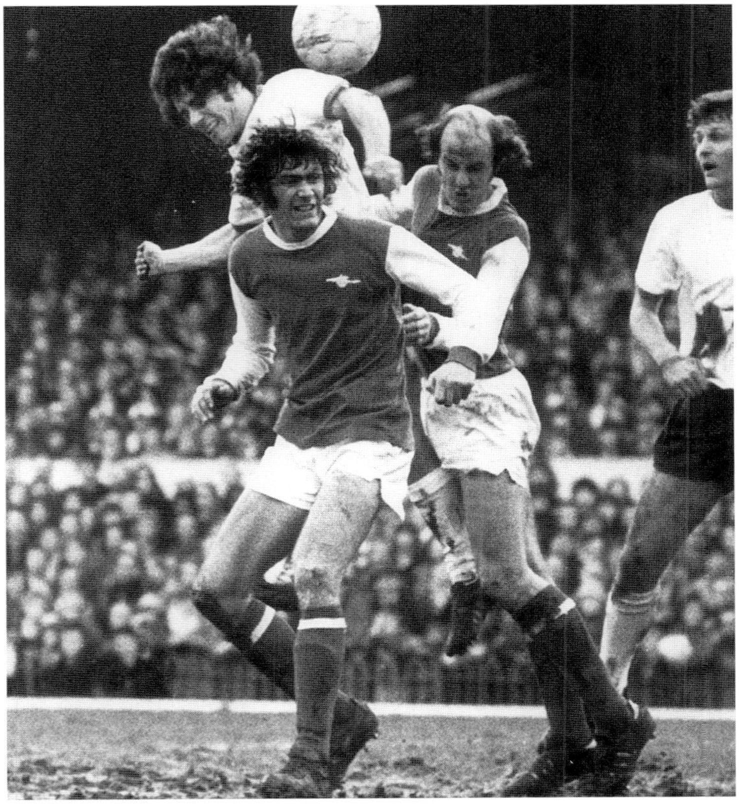

Arsenal's Brian Kidd and Terry Mancini look on anxiously as their goalkeeper Jimmy Rimmer punches away from Liverpool's Phil Thompson at Highbury in February 1975. The Arsenal number seven is George Armstrong. The Gunners won 2-0, both goals coming from Alan Ball, one of them from the penalty spot.

Liverpool's Kevin Keegan gets between Terry Mancini and Peter Simpson.

Bob Paisley had the hardest act in football to follow in succeeding the legendary Bill Shankly at Anfield. He did it the best way possible – by continuing to win championships and cups.

Ipswich Town's George Burley takes the ball away as Kevin Keegan looks back. Ipswich beat the Reds 2-0 at Portman Road in September 1975.

Ray Clemence blocks a shot at Upton Park in January 1976, when Liverpool won 4-0 and John Toshack scored a hat-trick.

Former Arsenal player Ray Kennedy, now playing for Liverpool, shields the ball from the Gunners' Trevor Ross at Highbury in November 1976. The game ended 1-1.

Steve Heighway in action against Crystal Palace at Anfield in January 1977, in the FA Cup third-round tie. The game ended goalless but Liverpool won the replay at Selhurst Park to set themselves on the road to Wembley.

Liverpool's Joey Jones gets above Peter Eastoe of Queen's Park Rangers at Loftus Road in May 1977. Liverpool were 1-0 down at half-time but Jimmy Case's goal gave them a point. Although they drew two and lost one of their last three games, the Reds still finished champions.

David Fairclough was known as 'Super Sub', thanks to his happy knack of coming on and scoring vital goals. He scored 52 goals altogether in 150 appearances – 62 of them as a substitute. He joined Liverpool as an apprentice in 1974 and left for Swiss football in 1982-83, before returning to England to play for Norwich and Oldham.

David Fairclough scores Liverpool's third goal six minutes from the end of the European Cup third-round tie against St Etienne at Anfield in March 1977. Liverpool won 3-1 on the night and 3-2 on aggregate.

Tommy Smith (4) scores with a header in the 1977 European Cup Final against Borussia Moenchengladbach in Rome. The Reds lifted the trophy with a 3-1 victory over the West German champions.

Phil Neal's penalty makes it 3-1 for Liverpool against Borussia Moenchengladbach in Rome.

Phil Neal joined Liverpool in 1974, for £65,000 from Northampton Town, to begin a remarkable career at Anfield. In 1985 he was appointed player-manager of Bolton Wanderers and could look back on 635 senior appearances and 60 goals for the Reds. He was capped 50 times for England and when Graham Taylor was England boss, Neal was his assistant. Between December 1974 and September 1983, Neal made 365 consecutive appearances for Liverpool, a club record.

David Fairclough gets the ball across despite the close attention of Manchester United's Jimmy Nicholl at Old Trafford in October 1977. United beat the champions 2-0.

Phil Neal scores from the penalty spot at Stamford Bridge in March 1978. It was not enough to save the Reds, however, who went down 3-1.

Ray Kennedy powers a header for Liverpool's first goal against Borussia Moenchengladbach in the 1978 European Cup semi-final second leg at Anfield. The Reds won 3-0 on the night and 4-2 on aggregate to reach another European Final where they beat FC Bruges 1-0 at Wembley.

A Graeme Souness shot goes just wide of the Bruges goal in the 1978 European Cup Final.

A 65th-minute chip-shot from Kenny Dalglish clinches the European Cup for Liverpool in 1978.

In 1978-79, Liverpool went out of the European Cup at the first hurdle – to Nottingham Forest of all clubs. Liverpool lost 2-0 at the City Ground and drew 0-0 at Anfield. Here, Garry Birtles puts Brian Clough's side ahead in the first game. Tony Woodcock, Ray Clemence, Phil Thompson and Emlyn Hughes (partly hidden) are the other players.

Kenny Dalglish joined Liverpool from Celtic, for £440,000 in 1977. He had already won 47 caps for Scotland and added 55 with Liverpool. He was only the second player ever to score 100 League goals in both Scotland and England. Dalglish hit 168 in all games for Liverpool – he made 494 senior appearances in all – and as player-manager immediately led the Reds to a League and FA Cup double.

Emlyn Hughes (6) looks back to see Forest's second goal on its way into the Liverpool net.

QPR's Hollins and Clement get in a tangle and Steve Heighway takes advantage to open the scoring at Loftus Road in November 1978. Liverpool went on to win 3-1 and at the end of the season were champions again.

Liverpool's Ray Clemence, Emlyn Hughes and Alan Hansen look on in horror as Joe Jordan (extreme right of picture) equalises for Manchester United in the FA Cup semi-final at Maine Road in March 1979. Liverpool lost the replay at Goodison Park 1-0.

Alan Hansen (6) scores an 82nd-minute equaliser through a crowded United defence at Maine Road.

Alan Hansen spent 14 glorious years with Liverpool, formed a great defensive partnership with Mark Lawrenson in the early 1980s, and won a host of club honours as well as 26 Scotland caps before a knee injury forced his retirement in 1991. Hansen joined the Reds in 1977, from Partick Thistle for £100,000. He made well over 550 senior appearances for Liverpool.

Mark Lawrenson joined Liverpool from Brighton for £900,000 in 1981 and teamed up with Alan Hansen at the centre of the Reds' defence. He won 38 caps for the Republic of Ireland, being qualified through his father, and made 341 first-team appearances for Liverpool before retiring through injury in 1988.

Ray Kennedy of Liverpool hooks the ball past Arsenal's Willie Young during the FA Cup semi-final third replay at Highfield Road, Coventry, in May 1980. After a draw at Hillsborough and two stalemates at Villa Park, Arsenal won this fourth game 1-0.

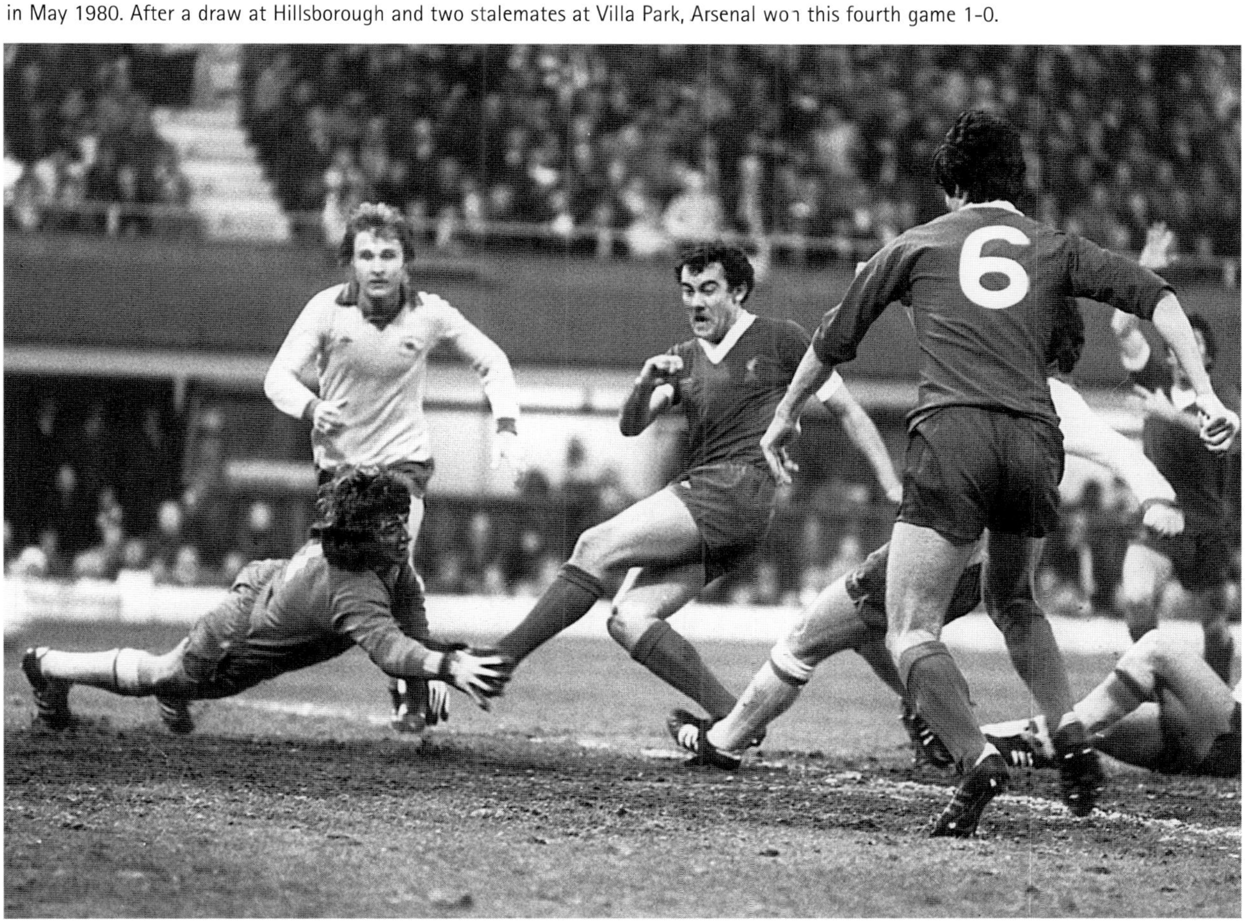

Ray Kennedy beats Pat Jennings at Highfield Road but his shot went wide.

Phil Thompson kisses the trophy after Liverpool's 4-1 win over Aston Villa at Anfield in May 1980 secured yet another League championship for the Reds. Thompson, a Liverpool fan when he was a schoolboy, signed for the club in 1971 and went on to make 466 senior appearances, scoring 12 goals. He was capped 42 times for England. He was transferred to Sheffield United in 1985.

Ray Kennedy was Bill Shankly's last signing for Liverpool when he signed from Arsenal for £180,000 in the 1974 close season. He had played at inside-forward in the Gunners' 1970-71 double team. In midfield for Liverpool, Kennedy made 384 senior appearances, scoring 72 goals, and played 17 times for England. In 1982 he was transferred to Swansea for £160,000.

This time Graeme Souness, Alan Hansen and Kenny Dalglish celebrate another title after the win over Villa.

Phil Thompson lifts another trophy, this time the European Cup won by Liverpool after they beat Real Madrid 1-0 in Paris in 1981.

Liverpool celebrate with the League Cup in 1982, after beating Spurs at Wembley. Back row (left to right): Mark Lawrenson, David Fairclough, Alan Hansen, Ronnie Whelan, Ian Rush, Bruce Grobbelaar, Bob Paisley (manager). Front row: Craig Johnston, Kenny Dalglish, Phil Neal, Graeme Souness, Sammy Lee, Alan Kennedy.

Sammy Lee joined Liverpool as an apprentice in 1976 and scored on his debut, against Leicester City, two years later. In 1986 he moved to QPR after 286 senior appearances and 19 goals for the Reds. Lee, who was capped 14 times for England, later joined the Anfield coaching staff.

Ronnie Whelan celebrates after scoring Liverpool's third goal against Tottenham Hotspur at Anfield in May 1982. The Reds were on the way to another League title. Ronnie Whelan signed for Liverpool from Irish football in 1979. He played in 495 first-team games for the Reds, scoring 73 goals, before moving to Southend United on a free transfer in 1994.

Champions again! Kenny Dalglish and skipper Graeme Souness parade the League championship trophy after the Reds beat Tottenham Hotspur 3-1 at Anfield in May 1982.

Bruce Grobbelaar made 628 senior appearances in Liverpool's goal. Born in Durban, South Africa, he joined the Reds from Crewe Alexandra for £250,000 in 1981, when he was also playing for Vancouver Whitecaps. Grobbelaar, an 'eccentric' goalkeeper, was a Zimbabwean international. He left Anfield in August 1994 and played for a succession of clubs. He was involved in a high-profile libel action after it was claimed he had been involved in contriving the results of some matches.

More Trophies Under Fagan

Joe Fagan, the former Manchester City centre-half who was now assistant manager at Anfield, took over from Bob Paisley for the start of the 1983-84 season and simply took over where Paisley had left off.

Ian Rush's shot hit the Everton post with Neville Southall well beaten at Anfield in November 1983. But the ball rebounded to Michael Robinson who made it 2-0. Liverpool went on to win 3-0.

Goalscorers Ian Rush and Michael Robinson celebrate after the Reds' victory in the Merseyside derby in November 1983.

Off the mark. John Wark is congratulated by Kenny Dalglish after scoring his first goal for Liverpool, against Watford at Vicarage Road in March 1984. Liverpool won 2-0 and were on their way to yet another championship

Wark in action with Watford's John Barnes trailing behind. Barnes later joined Liverpool.

Ian Rush takes the ball past Manchester United's Paul McGrath in the 1985 FA Cup semi-final at Goodison Park. The game ended 2-2 but Liverpool lost the replay at Maine Road 2-1.

Craig Johnston was born in South Africa but played for Sydney City in Australia before joining Middlesbrough. In April 1981 he signed for Liverpool and went on to make 260 first-team appearances (36 as a sub) and score 39 goals before quitting League football at the end of 1988-89 because of a family problem in Australia.

Dalglish Does the Double

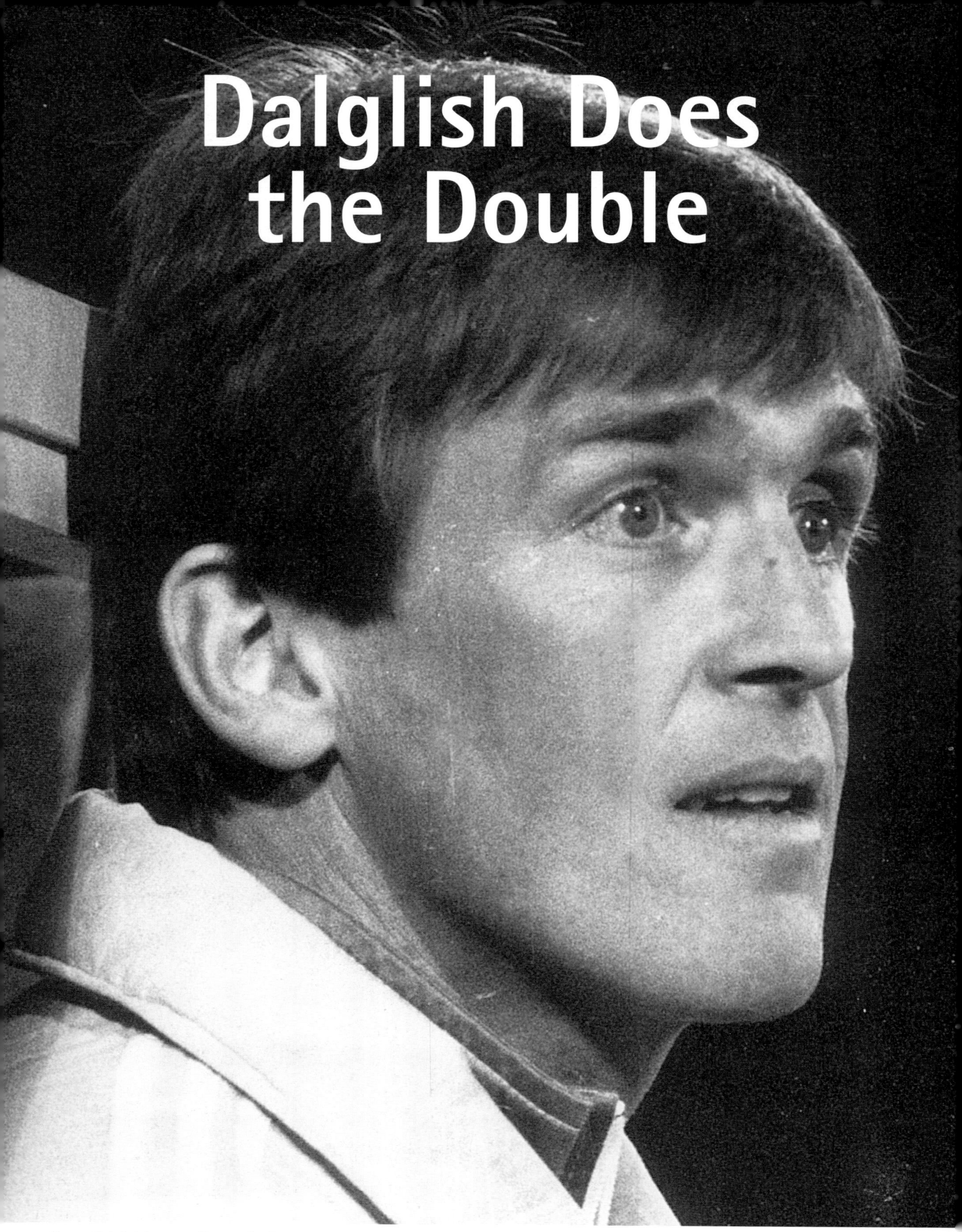

Kenny Dalglish became Liverpool's first player-manager when he stepped up to replace the retiring Joe Fagan in 1985. Dalglish responded by steering Liverpool to the League and FA Cup double.

Former Everton midfielder Steve McMahon was Kenny Dalglish's first signing as Liverpool manager when he bought him from Aston Villa for £350,000 in September 1985. He was capped 17 times for England. McMahon made 279 senior appearances for the Reds, scoring 50 goals, before moving to Manchester City in 1991.

Danish-born Jan Molby joined Liverpool from Ajax Amsterdam in 1984, for £575,000, and made 295 senior appearances, scoring 61 goals. He moved to Swansea City in 1996, after loan spells at Norwich and Barnsley.

Peter Beardsley joined Liverpool for £1.9 million from Newcastle in the 1987 close season, at that time a British record fee. Beardsley career had earlier looked to be foundering before Newcastle rescued him from the North American Soccer League. For Liverpool, Beardsley scored 59 goals in 177 senior games before moving to Everton in September 1991. He later rejoined Newcastle. He was capped 59 times for England.

Big Scottish defender Gary Gillespie joined Liverpool from Coventry City in 1983. After 212 senior appearances he moved to Celtic in August 1991. He scored a hat-trick against Birmingham City in April 1986.

Ian Rush scores the only goal of the game at the Baseball Ground on Boxing Day 1988. Peter Shilton looks back as the ball enters his net.

Ian Rush cost Liverpool £300,000 when Bob Paisley signed him from Chester in 1980. It was one of the best investments the club ever made. In two spells with the Reds, punctuated by a short stay with Juventus, Rush proved a remarkable goalscorer. It gave him Liverpool records for most goals in all games – 336 in 645 – most FA Cup goals, and most European goals until Michael Owen passed the tally. He finally left Anfield in 1996 and wound down his career with Leeds, Newcastle, Sheffield United and Wrexham.

John Barnes was signed for Liverpool by Kenny Dalglish in the 1987 close season, from Watford for £900,000. The following year he was voted Footballer of the Year. He left Anfield for Newcastle in 1997, after 409 senior appearances and 108 goals. He was capped 79 times for England and is perhaps best remembered for the goal he scored against Brazil in the Maracana Stadium in 1984.

In April 1991, Liverpool won a nine-goal thriller at Elland Road. Here David Speedie scores one of Liverpool's five goals.

Graeme Souness joined Liverpool from Middlesbrough for £350,000 in 1978. He made 352 first-team appearances and scored 56 goals before being transferred to Sampdoria for £650,000 in 1984. Souness later became player-manager of Rangers and then returned to take over at Anfield in April 1991 after Kenny Dalglish had surprisingly quit. The following season the club won the FA Cup but finished sixth in the League. In April 1992 Souness underwent a triple heart bypass operation and Ronnie Moran took over for a while. In 1994 Souness was replaced by Roy Evans.